Spot the Difference

Stems

Charlotte Guillain

www.heinemann.co.uk/library
Visit our website to find out more information about Heinemann Library books.

To order:
☎ Phone 44 (0) 1865 888066
▤ Send a fax to 44 (0) 1865 314091
▢ Visit the Heinemann Bookshop at www.heinemann.co.uk/library to browse our catalogue and order online.

First published in Great Britain by Heinemann Library,
Halley Court, Jordan Hill, Oxford OX2 8EJ, part of Harcourt Education. Heinemann is a registered trademark of Harcourt Education Ltd.

Editorial: Sian Smith and Cassie Mayer
Design: Joanna Hinton-Malivoire
Picture research: Erica Martin and Hannah Taylor
Production: Duncan Gilbert

Printed and bound in China by South China Printing Co. Ltd

ISBN 978 0 431 19229 1

12 11 10 09 08
10 9 8 7 6 5 4 3 2 1

British Library Cataloguing in Publication Data
Guillain, Charlotte
  Stems. - (Spot the difference)
  1. Stems (Botany) - Juvenile literature
  I. Title
  581.4'95

Acknowledgements
The publishers would like to thank the following for permission to reproduce photographs: ©FLPA pp.**14**, **22 right** (Chris Mattison), **6**, **17** (Nigel Cattlin), **11**, **23b** (Silvestris Fotoservice); ©Getty Images p.**10** (Photographer's Choice/ Grant Faint); ©istockphoto.com pp.**4 bottom right** (Stan Rohrer), **4 top left** (Chen Ping-Hung), **4 top right** (John Pitcher), **15**, **23 top** (rion819), **4 bottom left** (Vladimir Ivanov); ©Nature picture library pp.**20** (Jason Ingram), **13** (Philippe Clement); ©Photolibrary pp.**8** (Image Source Limited), **16** (Botanica /Sklar Evan), **19** (Jason Ingram), **7** (Michael Diggin), **9**, **22 left** (Pacific Stock), **21** (Plainpicture Gmbh & Co Kg), **18** (Susie Mccaffrey); ©Science photo library pp.**5** (Adam Jones), **12** (Maria & Bruno Petriglia).

Cover photograph of sunflowers reproduced with permission of ©Science Photo Library (Jeff Lepore). Back cover photograph of a strawberry runner reproduced with permission of ©Photolibrary (Botanica /Sklar Evan).

Every effort has been made to contact copyright holders of any material reproduced in this book. Any omissions will be rectified in subsequent printings if notice is given to the publishers.

Contents

What are plants?

Plants are living things.
Plants live in many places.

Plants need air to grow.
Plants need water to grow.
Plants need sunlight to grow.

What are stems?

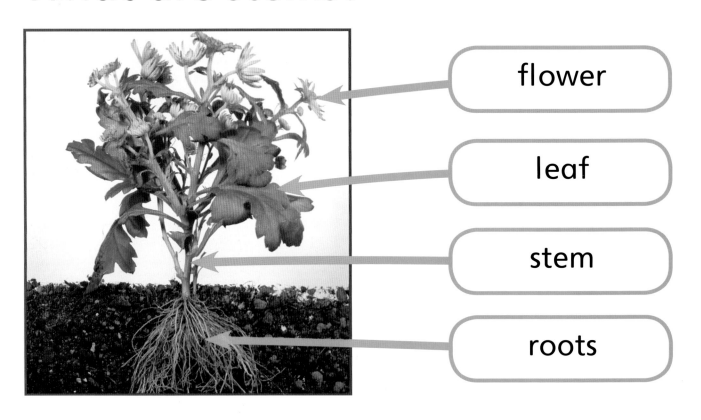

flower

leaf

stem

roots

Plants have many parts.
A stem is a part of a plant.

Most plants have stems.

Different stems

stem

This is a buttercup.
Its stem is short.

This is a sunflower.
Its stem is long.

9

stem

This is a redwood tree.
Its stem is thick.

10

This is a bean plant.
Its stem is thin.

This is a burnet.
It has one stem.

This is lavender.
It has many stems.

Amazing stems

spike

This is a cactus.
Its stem has thin spikes.

This is a rose.
Its stem has thick spikes.

stem

This is a strawberry plant.
Its stem grows along the ground.

This is an ivy plant.
Its stem grows along other plants.

This is a dogwood plant.
Its stem is red.

This is a golden willow.
Its stem is yellow.

What do stems do?

Stems hold leaves above the ground.

Stems carry water to
the leaves.

Spot the difference!

How many differences can you see?